creepy creatures

CONTENTS

Published by Creative Education
P.O. Box 227, Mankato, Minnesota 56002
Creative Education is an imprint of
The Creative Company
www.thecreativecompany.us

Design and production by Ellen Huber
Art direction by Rita Marshall
Printed by Corporate Graphics
in the United States of America

Photographs by 123RF (Adrian Hillman, Inzyx, Pavel
Konovalov), Alamy (MI (Spike) Walker), Jean-Michel
Crouzet, Dreamstime (Cphoto, Mashe, Sytnom), Getty
Images (Casper Benson, Gay Bumgarner, Darlyne A.
Murawski, Tim Ridley, Studio 504, Wim Van Egmond),
iStockphoto (Evgeniy Ayupov, Matthew Cole, Eric Isselée,
Ursula Markiewicz, Viorika Prikhodko, Alasdair Thomson,
Tomasz Zachariasz), Sealord Photography, Shutterstock
(Jubal Harshaw, Dr. Morley Read, Carolina K. Smith, M.D.)

Library of Congress Cataloging-in-Publication Data
Bodden, Valerie.
Worms / by Valerie Bodden.
p. cm. — (Creepy creatures)
Summary: A basic introduction to worms, examining
where they live, how they grow, what they eat, and
the unique traits that help to define them, such as the
ability of some species to regenerate.
Includes index.
ISBN 978-1-58341-997-7
1. Worms—Juvenile literature. I. Title. II. Series.
QL386.6.B63 2011
592'.3—dc22   2009052523
CPSIA: 040110 PO1135

First Edition
9 8 7 6 5 4 3 2 1

worms

VALERIE BODDEN

CREATIVE EDUCATION

You are digging in the garden. Suddenly you see something brown wriggling away. You push the dirt aside to get a closer look. It is a worm!

Worms are thin animals with long, soft bodies that do not have any bones. Worms do not have legs, but some worms have stubby body parts that look like legs. Most worms do not have eyes. Some worms' bodies are made up of rings called segments.

Earthworms have bodies that are made up of segments

Some kinds of worms are so small that you cannot see them without a **microscope**. Others can be more than 100 feet (30.5 m) long! Many worms are brown, black, or red. Some worms that live in the ocean are yellow, orange, or pink.

The most colorful worms live in the water or on plants

There are thousands of kinds of worms. Earthworms live in the soil. Most ribbon worms live in the sea. They can grow to be very long.

Some ribbon worms can grow up to 100 feet (30.5 m) long

Worms can be found almost everywhere! They live in forests, meadows, and gardens. Some live in water. Worms have to watch out for **predators**. Birds, frogs, and fish all eat worms.

Some people put worms on hooks to catch fish

Most kinds of worms begin their lives in an egg. Earthworms lay their eggs in a **cocoon**. Baby earthworms look like small adult worms. Some small worms live only a few months. But some big kinds of worms can live for 50 years.

Paddle worms live in the water and attach their eggs to rocks (right)

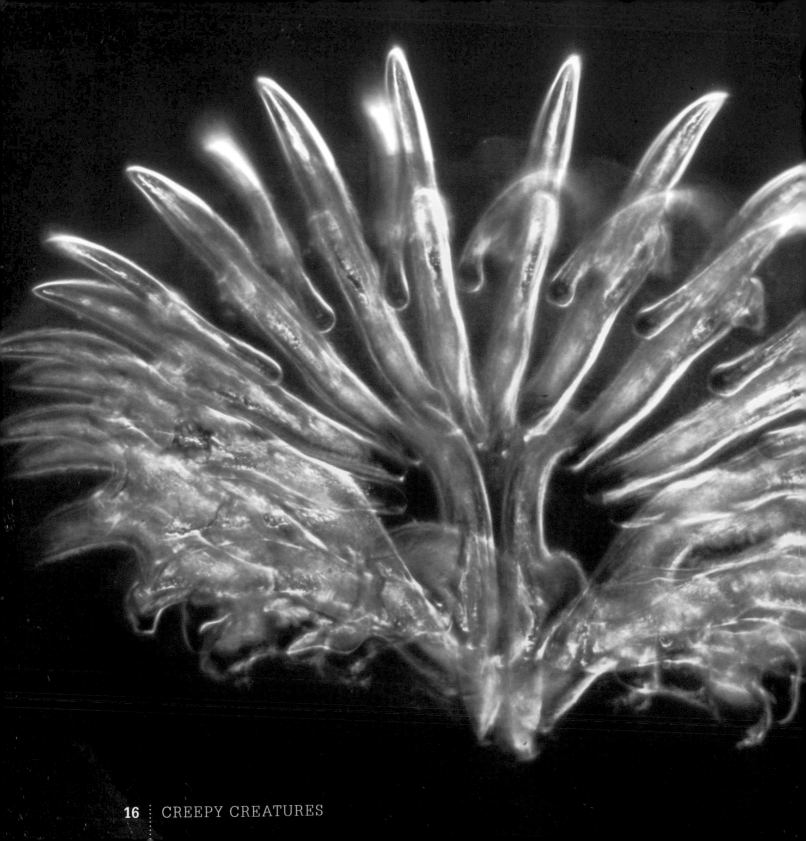

Some worms are **parasites**
(*PARE-uh-sites*). They live
inside animals or people.
They can make the animals or
people sick. Some worms kill
and eat other kinds of worms.
Many worms eat dead plants.

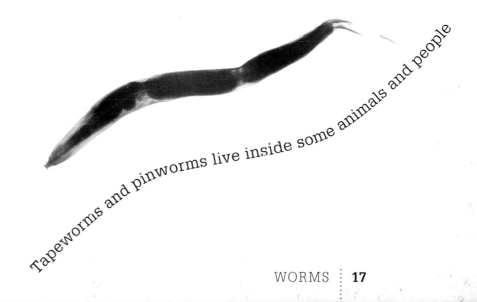

Tapeworms and pinworms live inside some animals and people

Some worms can regenerate (*ree-JEH-nuh-rate*). This means that if part of their body is cut off, it can grow back. Some kinds of worms can even split themselves in half and regenerate to make two worms!

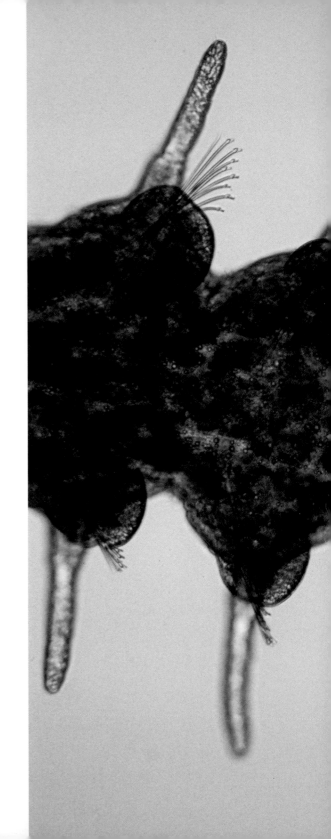

This close-up photo shows a bristle worm splitting into two

Earthworms make holes in the soil, letting in air and water

Long ago, people in Egypt believed that worms were **sacred**. Today, some people buy worms to put in their gardens. The worms help make the soil **fertile** (*FER-til*). It can be fun finding and watching these wriggly creepy creatures!

MAKE A WORM

You can make your own worm with a pipe cleaner and beads! First slide a bead to the middle of your pipe cleaner. Bend the pipe cleaner in half. Hold the two ends of the pipe cleaner together and slide another bead over them. Keep adding beads until your worm is completely covered. When you are done, twist the ends of your pipe cleaner together. Bend your worm into a wiggly shape!

GLOSSARY

cocoon: a special covering that keeps worm eggs safe until they hatch

fertile: good for growing plants

microscope: a machine that makes something look much bigger than it really is

parasites: plants or animals that live on or in other plants or animals and take food from them

predators: animals that kill and eat other animals

sacred: having to do with something that people worship or praise

READ MORE

Llewellyn, Claire, and Barrie Watts. *Earthworms*. New York: Franklin Watts, 2002.

Pfeffer, Wendy. *Wiggling Worms at Work*. New York: HarperCollins, 2004.

WEB SITES

The Adventures of Herman
http://urbanext.illinois.edu/worms/
Follow "Squirmin' Herman" the worm to learn more about worms.

Yucky Worm World
http://yucky.discovery.com/flash/worm/
Read about earthworms and find out how they make the soil fertile.